Going to GLACIER
National Park

By Alan Leftridge

D1306595

FARCOUNTRY
PRESS

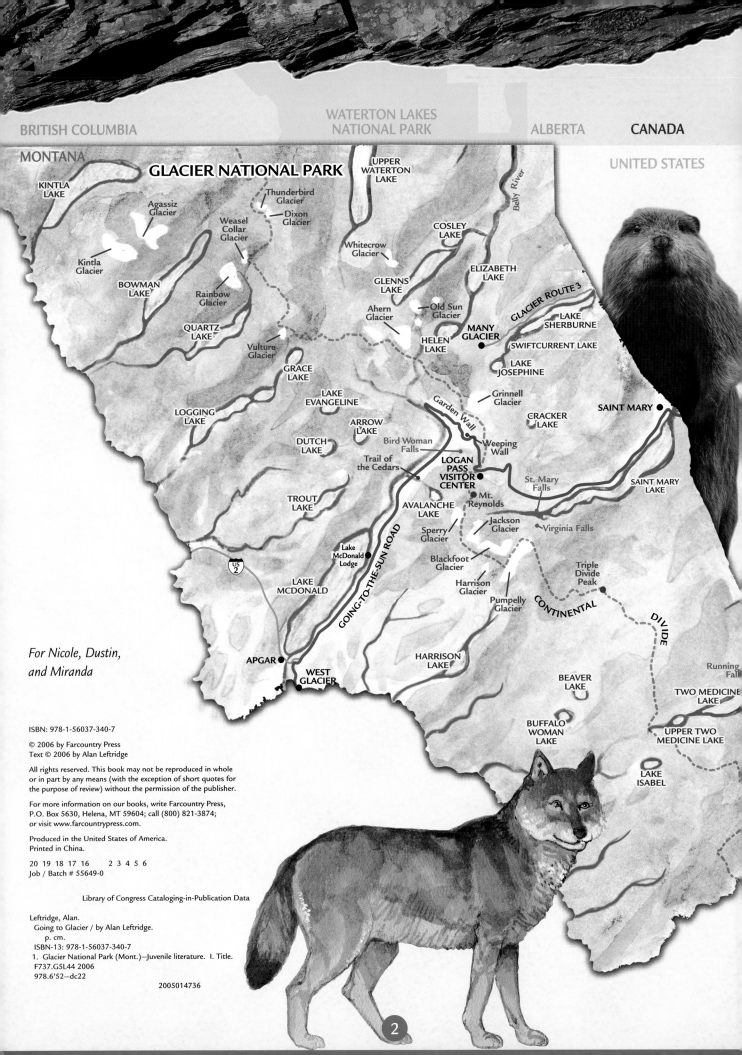

GLACIER NATIONAL PARK

BRITISH COLUMBIA

WATERTON LAKES NATIONAL PARK

ALBERTA

CANADA

MONTANA

UNITED STATES

KINTLA LAKE

Agassiz Glacier

Thunderbird Glacier

Dixon Glacier

Weasel Collar Glacier

Kintla Glacier

BOWMAN LAKE

Rainbow Glacier

QUARTZ LAKE

Vulture Glacier

GRACE LAKE

LOGGING LAKE

LAKE EVANGELINE

ARROW LAKE

DUTCH LAKE

Trail of the Cedars

TROUT LAKE

Lake McDonald Lodge

LAKE MCDONALD

US 2

APGAR

WEST GLACIER

GOING-TO-THE-SUN ROAD

UPPER WATERTON LAKE

Whitecrow Glacier

GLENNS LAKE

Ahern Glacier

COSLEY LAKE

ELIZABETH LAKE

Old Sun Glacier

MANY GLACIER

HELEN LAKE

Belly River

GLACIER ROUTE 3

LAKE SHERBURNE

SWIFTCURRENT LAKE

LAKE JOSEPHINE

Grinnell Glacier

Garden Wall

CRACKER LAKE

SAINT MARY

Bird Woman Falls

Weeping Wall

LOGAN PASS VISITOR CENTER

Mt. Reynolds

St. Mary Falls

SAINT MARY LAKE

AVALANCHE LAKE

Jackson Glacier

Virginia Falls

Sperry Glacier

Blackfoot Glacier

Harrison Glacier

Pumpelly Glacier

CONTINENTAL

Triple Divide Peak

DIVIDE

Running Fall

HARRISON LAKE

BEAVER LAKE

TWO MEDICINE LAKE

BUFFALO WOMAN LAKE

UPPER TWO MEDICINE LAKE

LAKE ISABEL

For Nicole, Dustin, and Miranda

ISBN: 978-1-56037-340-7

© 2006 by Farcountry Press
Text © 2006 by Alan Leftridge

For more information on our books, write Farcountry Press, P.O. Box 5630, Helena, MT 59604; call (800) 821-3874; or visit www.farcountrypress.com.

Produced in the United States of America.
Printed in China.

20 19 18 17 16   2 3 4 5 6
Job / Batch # 55649-0

Library of Congress Cataloging-in-Publication Data

Leftridge, Alan.
  Going to Glacier / by Alan Leftridge.
    p. cm.
  ISBN-13: 978-1-56037-340-7
  1. Glacier National Park (Mont.)—Juvenile literature. I. Title.
  F737.G5L44 2006
  978.6'52—dc22

                    2005014736

TABLE OF CONTENTS

Saint Mary Lake

Bald eagle

YOU'RE INVITED

to explore
Glacier National Park

WHEN? All year long

WHERE? Montana, USA, and
Alberta, Canada

WHAT TO BRING? Camera,
hiking boots, Junior
Ranger materials, and
this book

No RSVP necessary

The purpose of this book is to introduce you to the beautiful plant and animal life, dramatic weather, awesome geology, and some of the cultural influences that have molded Glacier National Park.

"The American Alps," "The Backbone of the World," the "Crown of the Continent"—Glacier National Park has been called all of these. After your visit to Glacier, you can come up with your own way of describing the park. Glacier is too big and too beautiful to be experienced in just one visit. It is my hope that *Going to Glacier* adds to your enjoyment and understanding of the park and encourages you to return many times.

So grab your camera, get your Junior Ranger materials close, and tighten your hiking-boot laces. The plant, animal, and geological wonders of Glacier National Park are here for you to discover and to excite your senses!

—*Alan Leftridge, author*

Welcome to
Glacier National Park!

LIKE NO OTHER PLACE ON EARTH

Glacier National Park, established in 1910, is a high-mountain park that excites all of your five senses and sets your imagination free. Glacier's majestic, awesome scenery includes towering mountain peaks that scrape the sky, lush forests, glacial-carved valleys, frigid lakes, rushing waterfalls, beautiful wildflower meadows, abundant wildlife, refreshing mountain air, rolling prairie grasslands, and dramatic mountain weather.

The American Alps

Once referred to as the American Alps, Glacier National Park preserves 1,013,572 acres (566,580 hectares) of some of the most spectacular glaciated landscape in North America. The park has the largest grouping of glaciers in the lower United States. Glacier has 175 peaks that are named, 6 of which are more than 10,000 feet (3,048 meters) in elevation.

WATCH FOR ANIMALS!

One Peak, Three Oceans

Triple Divide Peak, between Saint Mary and Cut Bank, is the only place in the United States where water flows to three different oceans. At Triple Divide Peak, water will enter the Columbia River system to the west and flow into the Pacific Ocean, or enter the Mississippi River system to mix with the Atlantic Ocean, or it will flow to Hudson Bay in Canada and end up in the Arctic Ocean.

A Hiker's Park

Triple Divide Peak is one of many destinations hikers choose to visit. Known as a hiker's park, Glacier has more than 700 miles (1,120 kilometers) of maintained trails.

Triple Divide Pass and Peak

EXPLORE!

As you explore Glacier National Park, you will experience about six different environments:

- the alpine zones
- the subalpine zones
- the aspen parklands
- the waters
- North Fork Valley
- McDonald Creek Valley

LOOK!

You can see Triple Divide Peak from an automobile pullout along the Going-to-the-Sun Road near Saint Mary.

Watchable Wildlife

Glacier is well known for its many wild creatures that are easy to see, whether you travel by foot along a trail, or by car. As a complete ecosystem, the Glacier area is home to all the predators and prey animals that existed here when our nation was established. Today, as in the past, it is the perfect place for biologists and vacationers to watch the animals in their daily routines.

Glacier's animals, plants, lakes, streams, and mountains have had unique importance throughout history. Kootenai, Kalispel, Salish (Flathead), Gros Ventre, and Blackfeet people have honored them for providing for their spiritual and survival needs.

White-tailed deer on trail to Camas Creek

The Waterton–Glacier Peace Park

Waterton Lakes National Park in Alberta, Canada, was established in 1895. Fifteen years later Glacier National Park was formed. In 1932, the same year that the Going-to-the-Sun Road was completed, Canada and the United States agreed to combine the two parks into the world's first International Peace Park.

At first, it was a signal to the world that Canada and the United States could solve their problems without war. Today, the idea of the peace park continues, and park managers from both countries work together to solve common problems.

Waterton-Glacier International Peace Park was designated as a World Heritage Site by the United Nations in 1995. The land that makes up the park has always held sacred meanings to the Blackfeet, Kootenai, and Salish people. Now it is also recognized as having a meaning of peaceful coexistence for all the people of the world.

As many as 2 million people visit Glacier National Park each year.

International Peace Park hike

GLACIER'S GLACIERS

You may have come to Glacier National Park to see the icy glaciers working, carving out valleys and reducing the mountains to rubble. Piedmont glaciers carved the park's major features of jagged mountains, U-shaped valleys, knife-like ridges, and big lakes. Those glaciers melted more than 12,000 years ago. This happened before there were records of humans living in the area. The glaciers in the park today were created in the last 400 years, with a growth spurt before the 1800s. They are grinding mountains and carving valleys—at their own pace. You will not see them working, because their movement is at the rate of one inch per year.

Grinnell Glacier

A Glacier is Born!

Glaciers begin when there is enough snowfall in winter so that in the warm summer months all the snow does not melt, blow away, or slide. Snow collected over several years becomes a snowfield. The snowfield turns into a glacier when snow on the bottom is squeezed by the weight of the new snow above. After many years, the snow at the bottom becomes pressed into ice, and the glacier begins to move downhill by the force of gravity.

DID YOU KNOW?

Most of the glaciers have shrunk to one-half or one-third the size they were 100 years ago. Others have disappeared altogether. In 1850, there were more than 150 glaciers in the park. At the present rate of melting, all of the glaciers will be gone by the year 2030.

Long Knife Peak

The Big Dozer

As a glacier moves downhill, it acts like a monstrous earthmoving machine. It pushes rocks in front of it, grinds rocks below, and gouges deep holes. In Glacier National Park, this process has carved the valleys, piled up earth to make rocky hills and ridges on the valley floor known as moraines, and dug depressions that become lakebeds. All of the lakes in Glacier National Park are the result of ancient glacial action.

Blue ice

As the Climate Changes

If snowfall increases, the glaciers will grow. Glaciers respond to long-term changes in weather known as climate. If the seasons become warmer or the winters become drier over many years, the glaciers will shrink. The climate of Glacier National Park has become warmer. The glaciers you see in the park are one-third to one-half the size they were 100 years ago. They may melt completely before you can return to the park with your children.

The Snow Park

It has been known to snow every month of the year in Glacier National Park, with most of the snowfall coming in January and February. Snow accumulations vary from a few inches in the southeastern part of the park to 50 feet at the high western elevations. That is as high as a 4-story building!

WATCH FOR SNOW!

Blue Ice

Glaciers crack open as they grow, leaving long crevices in the ice. These crevices expose long ice crystals. Sunlight strikes the crystals and the light is absorbed into the ice. The glacier appears blue because blue is the only color in the light spectrum that is reflected by the ice. The deepest blue color you see is sunlight reflected from the oldest, most squeezed ice.

Mount Clements in winter

Does anyone mind if I yodel?

JUST THE FACTS!

Glaciers are always changing. Currently, the largest glacier in the park is Blackfoot, with Harrison a close second.

GLACIER'S ACTION-PACKED GEOLOGY

The landscape you see in Glacier National Park was formed by events that started over one billion years ago. Three big events happened over a long period in order to make today's scenery.

1. rock formation ▶ 2. mountain building ▶ 3. landscape carving

How were the rocks formed?

The first great event happened about 1.5 billion years ago, when a shallow sea covered the area 50 miles (80 kilometers) west of the park. Around the sea, water runoff from the barren hills was rich in mud and sand. When seashell-dwelling animals died, the shells created lime deposits. These deposits of colored mud, sand, and lime remained there for hundreds of millions of years. As the years passed, the weight of increasingly new deposits pressed the earlier layers deeper towards the earth's mantle (the part of the earth that lies beneath the crust and above the central core). Pressure from above and heat from the mantle changed the mud, sand, and lime deposits into layers of colored rock. The sea dried and the layers of sedimentary rock lay undisturbed for about a billion years.

Where did the mountains come from?

The second event occurred about 60 million years ago, when much of the sedimentary rock from the seabed was pushed eastward as a gigantic 4-mile–thick (6.4-kilometer) slab of flat rock. The force that pushed the slab is known as plate tectonics. The slab was pushed up against a wall of rock that would not move. Plate tectonics pushed the slab over the unmoving rock layer, and after 5 to 10 million years, this formed the mountain range that makes up Glacier National Park. But the mountain range looked different than the one you see today. It took an ice age to sculpt the mountains of today's park.

SLOW-MOVING MOUNTAINS

What did the ice age do?

The last event started about 2 million years ago. The climate of the earth cooled, and enormous sheets of ice developed, extending as far south as present-day Montana.

A cap of ice (known as a piedmont glacier) covered Glacier's mountains to a depth of more than 1 mile (1.6 kilometers). Only the tallest peaks were not covered. With the force of gravity, this cap of ice scraped and carved the rock layers. The ice finally melted about 12,000 years ago, leaving the rugged landscape of mountains, lakes, rivers, and valleys that you enjoy today! It is this last ice age that glaciated the park.

In the past 10,000 years, little has happened to change the landscape. Rain, wind, rockslides, and the grinding effects of today's glaciers result in erosion that wears down the mountains at the rate of about 1 inch (2.5 centimeters) per year. That is about as much as your fingernails grow each year!

Glaciers Sculpt a Masterpiece

The geology of Glacier National Park includes arêtes, cirques, hanging valleys, horns, and moraines. All of these were made by the action of the long ago glaciers.

Mount Reynolds

Hanging valleys can be seen throughout Glacier National Park. Large glaciers carved the main valleys, while tributary glaciers worked the smaller side canyons. Unable to cut as deep as the valley glaciers, tributary glaciers left behind small "hanging" valleys on the mountainsides. Most of these valleys have a chain of lakes known as tarns. From these tarns, waterfalls tumble to the valleys below. Bird Woman Falls is a spectacular example of a waterfall from a hanging valley.

A **cirque** is a large bowl formed at the head of a glacier. When the ice melts, a small lake remains in the bowl left by the glacier. Avalanche Lake is an example of a cirque lake.

A **horn** is a nearly vertical mountain peak carved by several glaciers from different sides of the same mountain. Mount Reynolds at Logan Pass is a good example of a horn.

hanging valley
tarns
horn-shaped peak
cirque
horn
tributary glaciers
glacier
lateral moraine
arête
terminal moraine
U-shaped valley

Moraine on Heavens Peak

The Garden Wall

Moraines develop at the sides (lateral moraine) and front (terminal moraine) of a glacier. They are a mass of dirt and rock debris carried by a glacier. As the glacier melts, mounds of the debris are left behind as hills. Terminal moraines often serve as dams for lakes.

An **arête** (pronounced *uh-RATE*, a French word for "fi bone") forms when two glaci work on opposite sides of th same wall, leaving a long, narrow ridge. The Garden W is an arête separating the Many Glacier Valley from th McDonald Valley.

WHAT BROUGHT PEOPLE TO GLACIER?

MEXICO ←
CANADA →

The Old North Trail

People have roamed the Glacier area for at least 12,000 years. They may have been the ancestors of Native American tribes living near Glacier today. The Old North Trail was a well-known trail running north and south from Canada to Mexico 8,000 years ago.

When you are in Saint Mary, and the rumble of RVs and cars fades into the distance, listen for the silence and imagine the sounds of people with their dogs dragging travois over the ground headed for Mexico.

Many tribes used travois. They would place their belongings on the travois, two poles that a dog (in other areas, a horse) would drag as a tribe traveled.

Native Tribes and Mountain Men

The Glacier area was the exclusive home of Native American tribes such as the Blackfeet, Kalispel, Salish, and Kootenai people before the mountain men from Canada and the United States began moving into the area 300 years ago. These men came to trap beavers and other animals to export pelts to Europe, Canada, and the United States; the pelts were made into hats and clothing. The mountain men's arrival caused changes to the Native American ways of life. They brought with them diseases for which Native Americans had no immunity. The fur traders also introduced whiskey alcohol. Both caused great disruption to the Indian's traditional ways of living. Despite this, the Blackfeet, Salish, and Kootenai people continue to live and raise their families in the Glacier area.

Blackfeet Indian

11

Group of Salish Indians

Two Adventurers

In 1876, at the age of seventeen, James Willard Schultz left his home in New York and traveled to Montana to work at a trading post. He soon began living with the Blackfeet people and married a native woman. His new family gave him the name Apikuni, meaning "Far Off White Robe." Apikuni lived closely with his new family, even going with them on raids against other tribes. By the 1880s, he began writing about his experiences, telling stories that were published in books and in magazines like *Forest and Stream*.

It was an article published in *Forest and Stream* that captured the attention of its editor, George Bird Grinnell. The articles inspired Grinnell to tour the Glacier region with Schultz. With excitement, Grinnell visited the Glacier area and was shown the mountains, lakes, and glaciers by Apikuni. He was so impressed with what he called the "Crown of the Continent" that he too began writing about the wonders of Glacier. He soon began campaigning for it to be a national park.

Miners using sluice ramp

Gold!

Beginning in the 1860s, prospectors began combing the mountains looking for gold and silver. Mining claims were established in the mountains in the Swiftcurrent Valley, around Cracker Lake, Lake Josephine, and the Grinnell Valley. All of these areas were on the western portion of the Blackfeet Reservation. The U.S. government pressured the Blackfeet tribe into selling this portion of their reservation in 1895. This allowed the miners to search for the precious metals without being on reservation land. Even though the Blackfeet sold part of their homeland, the eastern area of Glacier holds great spiritual importance to the tribe—in much the same way as the western part of the park is of spiritual importance to Salish, Kalispel, and Kootenai tribes. It soon became clear that reports of precious metals in the mountains were exaggerated, and the mines were abandoned. A remnant of the mining era remains today: parts of a drilling rig are scattered at the head of remote Cracker Lake.

DID YOU KNOW?

George Bird Grinnell was a famous magazine editor and naturalist. General George Armstrong Custer asked Grinnell to come along on his 1876 military campaign to the Black Hills, in today's South Dakota. Grinnell decided not to go because of work duties at home. If he had gone, he may have been killed at the Battle of the Little Big Horn, and Glacier would have lost one of the people who later helped make it a national park.

James J. Hill

President William Howard Taft

George Bird Grinnell

Great Northern Railway

Many people came together over a 40-year period to establish Glacier as a national park and make it a popular destination. Access to Glacier National Park was difficult for tourists until the Great Northern Railway completed its transcontinental route across the northern United States. The route selected by President James J. "Empire Builder" Hill was over Marias Pass, and was completed in 1891. U.S. Highway 2 around the southern end of the park follows this transcontinental railway line. Hill's son, Louis, decided that the railroad should build hotels and chalets to attract tourists to the area.

Creation of the Park

Many people in the Flathead Valley decided that they wanted to see this special area protected. They rallied behind George Bird Grinnell and others supporting the creation of a national park. Four years later, in 1910, President William Howard Taft signed legislation making the area a national park. No longer could Glacier's wonders be exploited for the economic benefit of a few. From then on, Glacier was to be a preserved as a park, unimpaired, for all to enjoy.

The call of the Mountains
Vacations in **Glacier National Park**

Glacier national park

Promotional posters for Glacier National Park

JUST THE FACTS!

Although most people think of George Bird Grinnell as the father of Glacier National Park, army lieutenant John T. Van Orsdale first suggested it in a letter to Fort Benton's River Press in 1883.

George Bird Grinnell on Grinnell Glacier

What's in a Name?

Indian people gave names to all of the lakes, mountains, waterfalls, and streams. White people also named many of the features, some in honor of particular Indians. Some of these names and stories include:

SIYEH MOUNTAIN

CHIEF MOUNTAIN

George Bird Grinnell named Siyeh Mountain for a Blackfeet Indian. His people described him as being so reckless that none of his tribal members would go with him on raids against the enemy. Grinnell chose the name because "Sai-yeh" means Crazy Dog or Mad Wolf.

The present-day name of Chief Mountain is from the original Blackfeet Indian names of "Old Chief" or "The Mountain-of-the-Chief." Indian braves climbed the peak and stayed on the top until they experienced a spiritual dream. The most popular story of the mountain is about a Salish brave who risked discovery by Blackfeet enemies. He carried to the top a bison skull that he used as a pillow. The first white men to climb the mountain in 1892 discovered a weathered bison skull on the summit, a place that a bison could not have reached.

SINOPAH MOUNTAIN

The impressive Sinopah Mountain in the Two Medicine area means "kit fox" in the Blackfoot language. Sinopah was the Indian wife of Hugh Monroe, a white man known as Rising Wolf.

LAKE MCDONALD

Lake McDonald was once called Sacred Dancing Lake because the tribes gathered there for spiritual ceremonies every year.

LODGES: LIVIN' LARGE IN GLACIER

Imagine the excitement of visiting Glacier National Park in the 1920s. You arrive on a passenger train pulled by a huge fire-breathing steam locomotive. Blackfeet Indian tribal members dressed in buckskin regalia meet you at the East Glacier depot. You spend the night in "The Big Tree Lodge," as the Blackfeet called it, now called the Glacier Park Lodge. The following day, a sturdy horse carries you into the park, over a mountain pass to the Two Medicine Chalet. For six to ten days, you rode a horse, sailed by boat, and hiked to the lodges, chalets, and tent camps throughout the park.

Many Glacier Hotel

Granite Park Chalet

Lake McDonald Lodge

Sperry Chalet

Two Medicine Chalet

Belton Chalet

Glacier Park Lodge

Glacier lodges

DID YOU KNOW?

During his stay, President Roosevelt was made an honorary member of the Blackfeet tribe. He was given the name Lone Chief. First Lady Eleanor Roosevelt was given the name Medicine Pipe Woman.

Just call me Lone Chief.

President Franklin Roosevelt

The Two Medicine Chalet

The Two Medicine Camp Store is the only remaining structure of the Two Medicine Chalet complex. The store served as the main dining hall, built in 1915. Other buildings included a dormitory and cabins. Except for the main dining hall, all of the other buildings were removed during the winter of 1953.

When it was still the dining hall, the Two Medicine Camp Store was the site of a speech broadcast by President Franklin Roosevelt on August 5, 1934. In his speech, Roosevelt exclaimed, "Today for the first time in my life I have seen Glacier Park. Perhaps I can best express to you my thrill and delight by saying that I wish every American, both old and young, could have been with me today. The great mountains, the glaciers, the lakes, and the trees make me long to stay for the rest of the summer."

Two Medicine Chalet

Glacier Park

Glacier Park Lodge

Louis Hill of the Great Northern Railway Company told his architect to design the Glacier Park Lodge in East Glacier to look like a giant log cabin. This was going to be the first lodge visitors would see when they arrived by train from the east, so he wanted it to be impressive. It was impressive then, and it is today.

The hotel opened in 1913 with rooms costing from $2 to $5 per day, and that included breakfast! Guests enjoyed the indoor swimming pool, the massive tree columns in the lobby, and the indoor campfire circle.

Lake McDonald Lodge

John Lewis built the Lake McDonald Lodge. Built to look like a Swiss chalet on the outside, Lewis wanted it to look like a hunting lodge on the inside. It opened in 1914 and was originally called The Glacier Hotel. You will notice that the lakeside part of the lodge is what appears to be the main entrance. Before the Going-to-the-Sun Road was opened in 1932, the lakeside was the lodge's main entrance. Visitors arrived from Apgar on steamboats.

Lake McDona

Interior of Lake McDona

WHAT'S THE DIFFERENCE?

CHALET, LODGE, OR HOTEL?

A chalet is a Swiss-style house or cottage traditionally made of wood with wide overhanging eaves.

A lodge is a main building in a vacation complex providing meals and overnight accommodations.

A hotel is a lone building where people get meals and pay for overnight lodging.

Boat Emeline loaded with passengers

16

Belton Chalet

Like the Lake McDonald Lodge, the Belton Chalet was designed to look like a Swiss chalet. Built by the Great Northern Railway, it was meant to serve the western entrance to Glacier National Park. The chalet opened in 1910 with a night's lodging costing $2. Recently, there have been several accounts of friendly spirits who haunt the main building. There is no proof, though. You be the judge.

Belton Chalet

GHOST XING

Many Glacier Hotel

Back in 1915, room rates were $5 per night, which included meals. By the 1930s, Blackfeet Indians performed for guests during the days and National Park Service rangers gave lectures and showed films in the evenings. Harsh winter conditions in the Swiftcurrent Valley caused the hotel to need massive repairs to its roof, foundation, and walls. Major repairs were completed in 2005.

Many Glacier Hotel

Visitors ride horses through bear grass

For Hikers Only!

Roads were never built to the chalets deep in the Glacier wilderness. Two rustic chalets remain from the early days of Glacier that you cannot get to by car or boat. The Granite Park Chalet and the Sperry Chalet are two places you might have stayed the night in 1915 while touring Glacier by horseback. You can spend the night at either chalet, if you hike to them on trails well worn by horses and their riders of long ago. Reservations are required to stay in the chalets.

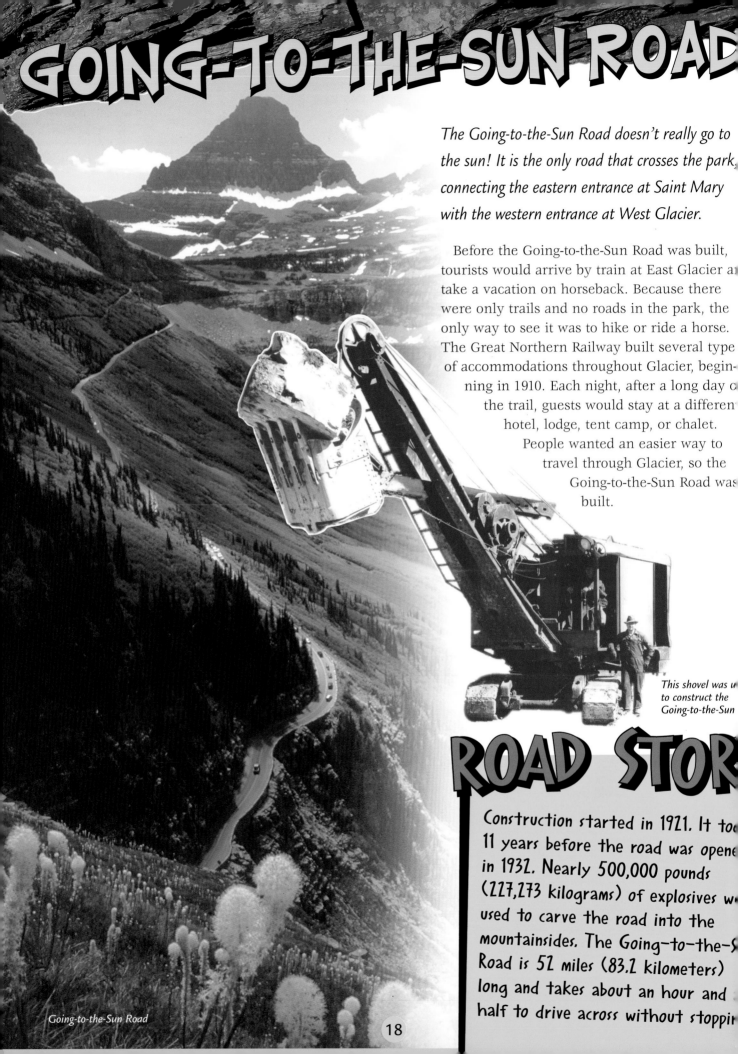

GOING-TO-THE-SUN ROAD

The Going-to-the-Sun Road doesn't really go to the sun! It is the only road that crosses the park, connecting the eastern entrance at Saint Mary with the western entrance at West Glacier.

Before the Going-to-the-Sun Road was built, tourists would arrive by train at East Glacier and take a vacation on horseback. Because there were only trails and no roads in the park, the only way to see it was to hike or ride a horse. The Great Northern Railway built several types of accommodations throughout Glacier, beginning in 1910. Each night, after a long day on the trail, guests would stay at a different hotel, lodge, tent camp, or chalet. People wanted an easier way to travel through Glacier, so the Going-to-the-Sun Road was built.

This shovel was used to construct the Going-to-the-Sun

ROAD STORY

Construction started in 1921. It took 11 years before the road was opened in 1932. Nearly 500,000 pounds (227,273 kilograms) of explosives were used to carve the road into the mountainsides. The Going-to-the-Sun Road is 52 miles (83.2 kilometers) long and takes about an hour and a half to drive across without stopping.

Going-to-the-Sun Road

The Divide

There are many places to stop and enjoy the beautiful scenery while traveling the Going-to-the-Sun Road, but the one stop that most people make is Logan Pass. A pass is a road or trail over or through mountains. There are thousands of passes through the Rocky Mountains. Logan Pass is special, because the view makes you feel like you are at the top of the world. The elevation at Logan Pass is 6,646 feet (2,020.4 meters) above sea level.

The Going-to-the-Sun Road, as it crosses Logan Pass, is the only road over the Continental Divide in Glacier National Park. The Continental Divide is the most elevated part of the Rocky Mountain range, running north and south.

Rain falling on the east side of the divide flows into the Atlantic Ocean and rain falling on the west side of the divide flows into the Pacific Ocean. Stand by the Logan Pass sign at the Going-to-the-Sun Road and have your picture taken with one foot on each side of the divide!

Logan Pass Visitor Center

Snowing on "the Sun"

Heavy snowfalls come early to Glacier. The Going-to-the-Sun Road normally closes during the third week of October, but it is kept open longer if the season is dry. Once it closes, it is free from vehicle traffic until the next spring.

Every April, work crews begin plowing the snow to open the road. They will often remove the equivalent of about 200 houses full of snow! The earliest date the road has opened was May 16 in 1987. The latest date the road has opened (because of weather) was June 28 in 2002.

The largest snowdrift that is removed every year is called "Big Drift," just east of Logan Pass. Big Drift is often 80 feet (24.3 meters) high, as tall as a seven-story building.

DEEP SNOW

Got any hot chocolate?

A party on horseback rides to Grinnell Glacier

JUST THE FACTS!

Before the Going-to-the-Sun road opened, the most popular way to see the park was on horseback.

Repairing guard wall at pull-out

The Loop
Logan Pass
Visitor Center
Trail of the Cedars
Sacred Dancing Cascade
Jackson
Glacier Overlook
Lake McDonald Lodge
Apgar Village

Saint M
Visitor Ce
GOING-TO-THE-SUN ROAD
Sun Point
Sunrift Gorg
Continental Divide

Great places to stop along the Going-to-the-Sun Road

The Road Gets a Facelift

You will often see road construction during your drive along the Going-to-the-Sun Road. The hard winter weather of snow, thawing and freezing, rock avalanches, as well as the increase in vehicle travel and the weight of those vehicles have damaged the road over time. Road crews will be reconstructing the road until 2012.

DON'T FORGET YOUR UMBRELLA

The Little Red Busses

The first busses appeared in Glacier in 1914. The roads were not yet paved and were in poor condition. Bus rides were rougher than being on horseback! The "Glacier Reds" that you see in the park today appeared in 1936. Glacier is the only national park that keeps a fleet of red busses running. The "Glacier Reds" travel all the paved roads in the park and have become a symbol of Glacier's history. Imagine what it must have been like to tour the park fifty years ago in one of them!

*A red bus drives p
the Weeping Wall*

WILDLIFE OF GLACIER

Welcome to Mountain Time—where the mountains, valleys, rivers, lakes, weather, and seasons shape the lives of the animals. More than 70 species of mammals live out their lives in this protected land.

Black Bear or Grizzly Bear?

Nature has painted the black bear and the grizzly bear with colors that make them hard to tell apart. All bears are dangerous, but grizzly bears are known to be very unpredictable.

Black bears can be black, cinnamon, brown, and nearly white. Grizzly bears can be yellowish, brown, nearly black, and almost white.

You can tell the difference by the noses and the shoulders of the bears. Black bears have a straight nose; grizzly bears have a dished nose. Grizzly bears have a large hump between their front shoulders; black bears do not. Make sure to identify bears at a safe distance.

GRIZZLY BEAR

BLACK BEAR

Huckleberries

Berries and Horsetails: A Bear Diet

Black bears and grizzly bears have similar diets. They both eat insects, berries, forbs (an herb other than grass), horsetails (a type of plant), grasses, and mammals.

They eat different foods in different seasons. In the spring, they eat a lot of grasses, horsetails, and forbs.

Insects are eaten mostly in the summer months. Berries make up a large part of their diet in the late summer and autumn. Huckleberries, in particular, are full of sugar and turn to fat that bears require for surviving their hibernation from November to April.

There are more than 200 grizzly bears and about 500 black bears in Glacier.

DID YOU KNOW?

All animals in Glacier National Park are wild and possibly dangerous. Do not approach animals. Observe all wildlife at a distance that does not change their behavior. This is for your safety and to keep from upsetting the animals.

Black bear

SAFETY ZONE

You might ask:

"Is it safe for me to hike in bear country?"

Yes, but there are always risks involved with being in their territory. Read and follow all the suggestions for hiking in bear country in pamphlets that are given out by park rangers when you entered Glacier. Look for updated information posted at trailheads. Avoid surprising a bear by being alert, hiking midday with a group, and making noise.

"But what if I run into a bear on a trail?"

There is no simple answer. Bears react differently to each situation. Here are some suggestions from hikers who have encountered bears:

- Never run! Instead, back away slowly.

- Talk quietly or not at all.

- Turn sideways, or bend at the knees to appear small.

- Avoid looking directly at the bear.

- Detour around the bear if you must go forward on the trail.

- If the bear attacks, use bear spray and protect your chest and abdomen by falling to the ground on your stomach, or curling up like a baby. Cover the back of your neck with your hands. Do not move until you are certain the bear has left.

- Remember, you are a guest in bear country. Be a good one!

Grizzly bear

Existing together

In the early 1900s, grizzly bears, mountain lions, lynx, bobcats, and gray wolves were killed in predator control programs. Park managers believed they threatened the animals that visitors came to the park to see: deer, moose, and elk.

Over time, managers learned that a balance of predator and prey is important to maintaining a healthy ecosystem in Glacier National Park. Predator control programs were phased out in the 1950s and 1960s to allow the predators to again live in Glacier National Park. This presence of predators keeps populations of prey such as hares, elk, deer, and moose from getting too large and destroying the forest by overeating.

DID YOU KNOW?

A grizzly bear may weigh half as much as your car, and it can sprint almost twice as fast as an Olympic runner!

Who's That Howlin'?

Wolves returned to the North Fork of the Flathead River Valley in the early 1980s. Park officials believe the wolves moved down from Canada. They prefer to eat small mammals and birds, but they also prey on young and diseased deer, moose, and elk. The largest concentration of wolves is in the North Fork area; the number of wolves in the park varies.

You probably won't see a wolf while you are in Glacier because they are secretive and travel mostly at night. Unlike being in grizzly bear territory, being in wolf territory is not dangerous. There is no documented case of a healthy wolf ever killing a human in North America.

Although you probably will not see a wolf, you can listen for one. The howl of the gray wolf can be heard from 10 miles (16.1 kilometers) away. As afternoon light fades in the North Fork Valley, listen for the long, sorrowful howl of the gray wolf. Its cry brings chills and reminds you that you are visiting a true American wilderness.

The Song Dog

It usually starts with one coyote howling in the night. In less than a minute, several more coyotes will join the chorus. The song dog of the West is numerous and lives in every part of the park up to timberline, the altitude at which trees cannot grow. You may even encounter a coyote trotting down a road in front of your car. Look for them in eastern grasslands hunting rodents. If you don't see a coyote, listen for its singing at night.

Yip, yip, yip!

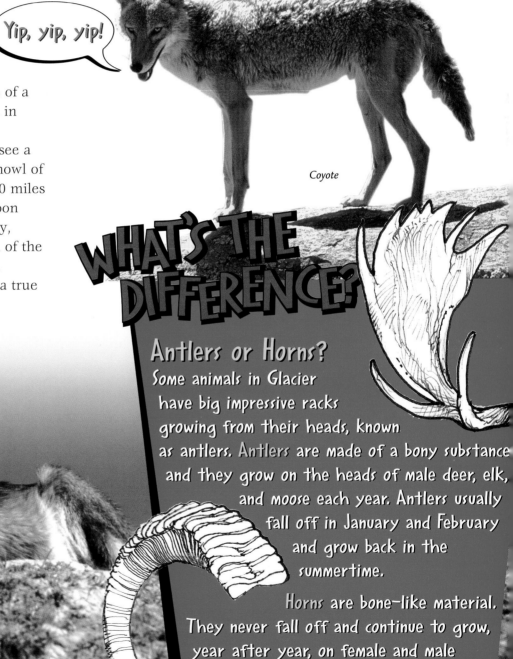

Coyote

WHAT'S THE DIFFERENCE?

Antlers or Horns?

Some animals in Glacier have big impressive racks growing from their heads, known as antlers. Antlers are made of a bony substance and they grow on the heads of male deer, elk, and moose each year. Antlers usually fall off in January and February and grow back in the summertime.

Horns are bone-like material. They never fall off and continue to grow, year after year, on female and male bighorn sheep and mountain goats.

23

Young moose

Moose: The Deer's Gawky Cousin

Easily identified by its large size, overhanging snout, and dangling "bell" of skin under its neck, the gawky moose is the largest member of the deer family.

Living up to 20 years on mountainsides and in lake areas, adult moose can swim as fast as two people paddling a canoe and can run as fast as the park's maximum speed limit of 45 miles per hour (72.42 kilometers per hour). Be careful where you choose to skip stones—moose love the water!

Elk

If it looks like a deer, but it is much larger than either a mule deer or a white-tailed deer, then it is an elk. They can be almost as large as a moose! The best time to see elk in Glacier National Park is in the autumn, when they migrate to the lower elevations around Saint Mary Lake and in the North Fork area. During the summer, they travel in small groups among the trees of the spruce forests. They can live up to 14 years in a wild protected place like Glacier National Park.

WATCH FOR BROWSERS

Bull elk

White-tailed Deer

You will recognize white-tailed deer by their long white tails, which they wave as a warning signal when frightened. They are browsers that eat vegetation growing in burned areas and in old beaver meadows. White-tailed deer are common in Glacier National Park and can live to be 16 years old. They can run up to 40 miles per hour (64.37 kilometers per hour) and leap distances of up to 30 feet (9 meters).

White-tailed deer

Mule Deer

Walt Disney selected the mule deer to be the beloved Bambi in his movie. It is the most common deer you will see in Glacier National Park. Larger than the white-tailed deer, it is recognized by the way it bounds on all four legs as it escapes from danger.

Mule deer

TIPPING THE SCALE

White-tailed de
50 to 400 poun
(22.7 to 181.8 kilogra

Mule deer:
125 to 400 poun
(56.8 to 181.8 kilogra

Elk:
500 to 1,000 pou
(110 to 220 kilograms)

Moose:
600 to 1,200 pour
(272.7 to 545.5 kilogr

Mountain goat

Mountain Goats

The mountain goat has been used as an unofficial emblem of Glacier National Park ever since the Great Northern Railway began using "Rocky the Great Northern Goat" as part of their advertising in 1915. Mountain goats are a common sight in the Logan Pass area and at Goat Lick turnout along U.S. Highway 2. Both male and female goats have black, slightly curved horns that are half the length of their head.

Two hoary marmots in a mock "boxing match"

"Whistle Pigs"

About the size of a soccer ball—with a tail—hoary marmots are the largest members of the squirrel family. They weigh from 8 to 20 pounds (3.6 to 9.1 kilograms). Living on rocky alpine slopes, in meadows, and along cliff faces throughout the park, these grizzly-looking colonial rodents are distinguished by their mock boxing matches, nuzzling of one another, sunbathing, and standing on their hind legs chirping out whistles. Commonly referred to as "whistle pigs," they fatten themselves during the summer on grasses, flowers, and herbs and burn off the fat in hibernation from September to June.

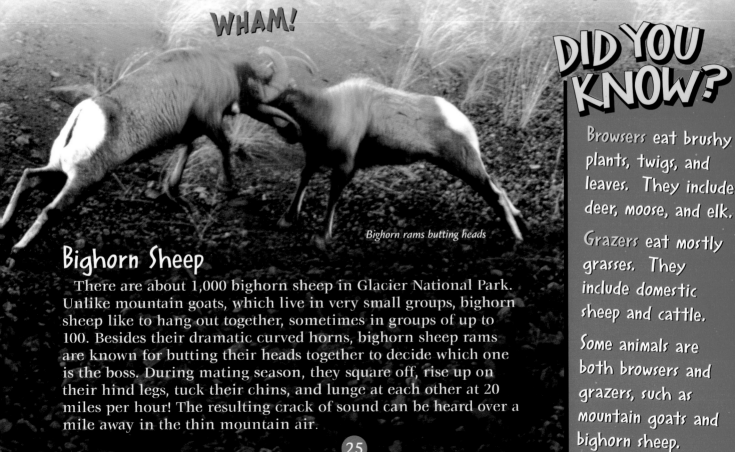

WHAM!

Bighorn rams butting heads

Bighorn Sheep

There are about 1,000 bighorn sheep in Glacier National Park. Unlike mountain goats, which live in very small groups, bighorn sheep like to hang out together, sometimes in groups of up to 100. Besides their dramatic curved horns, bighorn sheep rams are known for butting their heads together to decide which one is the boss. During mating season, they square off, rise up on their hind legs, tuck their chins, and lunge at each other at 20 miles per hour! The resulting crack of sound can be heard over a mile away in the thin mountain air.

DID YOU KNOW?

Browsers eat brushy plants, twigs, and leaves. They include deer, moose, and elk.

Grazers eat mostly grasses. They include domestic sheep and cattle.

Some animals are both browsers and grazers, such as mountain goats and bighorn sheep.

The Night is Alive!

The day draws to a close, the sky begins to darken, and you settle down for sleep. Then, out of the corner of your eye, you spot something zooming among the trees and across your campsite.

Northern flying squirrel

While you are getting ready for bed, many animals are just awakening. These animals that start the active part of their routine at night are known as nocturnal animals.

What you saw out of the corner of your eye was a nocturnal northern flying squirrel. With cape-like furred skin flaps stretching between their front and hind legs, flying squirrels are able to glide half the length of a soccer field from one tree to the next. They live in the same forests as red squirrels and, like the red squirrels, they do not hibernate. On cold days in Glacier National Park, you can find up to 10 flying squirrels snuggled to stay warm in an abandoned woodpecker hole.

No friend to the northern flying squirrel, the graceful furry marten prowls the forest looking for a meal that might include an unfortunate flying squirrel or a red squirrel sleeping in its den. Martens live far from civilization. But you might see one of these bushy-tailed predators scamper across the forest floor or climbing among tree branches if you spend the night in Glacier's backcountry.

Marten

SHHH! QUIET PLEASE

Red squirrel

Glacier's Acrobats

The red squirrel is the only tree squirrel in Glacier National Park. Locally known as the pine squirrel, these tree acrobats will delight you with their antics. You may detect pine squirrels by sight or sound. Their noisy chattering is a territorial cry. With a home range of less than two football fields and populations of 2 squirrels to 3 acres, their territories easily overlap. They do not like that and fight to protect their food of pine nuts and fungi. Red squirrels do not hibernate and can live 10 years if they stay away from owls, martens, foxes, and bobcats.

The Rip Van Winkle of Glacier

At Logan Pass, winter often lingers until June, and you may find patches of snow in August. It is here you will see Columbian ground squirrels. These colonial animals emerge from their hibernation in May. By August, they return to their annual slumber. They are only awake for 4 months! Watch for Columbian ground squirrels while you are visiting Logan Pass. They will probably not notice you; they are too busy eating grass and herbs, building up fat to burn off during their long winter's sleep.

Columbian ground squirrel

An Alpine Farmer

Like a farmer covering haystacks in a midsummer thunderstorm, the American pika stashes the alpine flowers and grasses it has cut in order to keep them dry. When the sun returns, the pika spreads the hay on rocks to dry. The hay is then stored deep within the rockslide for the pika to eat during the winter. Often called rock rabbits, you will hear their short bugle-like warning squeaks when you come near their rocky slope homes near alpine meadows. The size of a grapefruit, and with tiny ears, pikas live among the rocks. The pika does not hibernate but will stay active in the dark among the rocks under several feel of snow.

American pika

A CHECKLIST OF MAMMALS:

It may take you several trips to Glacier to see all of these animals. Start a checklist!

- ☐ American pika
- ☐ beaver
- ☐ bighorn sheep
- ☐ black bear
- ☐ bobcat
- ☐ chipmunk
- ☐ Columbian ground squirrel
- ☐ coyote
- ☐ elk
- ☐ golden-mantled ground squirrel
- ☐ gray wolf
- ☐ grizzly bear
- ☐ hoary marmot
- ☐ marten
- ☐ moose
- ☐ mountain goat
- ☐ mule deer
- ☐ red fox
- ☐ red squirrel
- ☐ white-tailed deer

Redhead of the Park

Any time of year, look for red foxes trotting about the edges of meadows looking for hares, ground squirrels, mice, and nesting birds. Notice how they seem to float above the ground with their long white-tipped tail trailing behind. They are easy to identify because no other animal in Glacier National Park is red, has a long bushy tail, weighs up to 15 pounds (6.8 kilograms), and reaches 3.5 feet (1meter) in total length. They are most active at night but they are sometimes seen during the daytime. Dog-like, red foxes are a distant cousin of the wolf and coyote.

Red fox

Bobcat

Beavers

Imagine building a dam across a flowing stream at night, without a light. That is what beavers can do. The ponds they make cause willows to grow along the shore. The willows become food for the beavers. Eventually their ponds fill in with silt and turn into meadows. The meadows become home to elk, deer, bobcats, and foxes. Look for the evidence of beavers throughout the low-lying stream valleys on the east side and west side of Glacier.

DAM UNDER CONSTRUCTIO

Beaver

Bobcats

These 35-pound (15.9-kilogram) short-tailed cats can easily capture small prey, like martens. Birds in their nests near the ground can also fall victim to bobcats as they roam the forests and meadows at night. Unlike your pet cat back home, bobcats enjoy water, making beavers a likely prey.

Mountain Lions

Widely distributed throughout North America, the mountain lion ha been given many names: puma, catamount, painter, cougar, and panth These large majestic cats can reach 150 pounds (68 kilograms) and feet (2.5 meters) in length. Mountain lions are common yet elusive. The chance of seeing a lion on your trip to Glacier is small. They usually hide when they detect humans. If you do see a mountain lion, you will probably do so from your car while the lion is crossing the road in the evening in the North Fork area. It difficult to ignore an animal that takes up half the roadway! Lions are easy to identify. They are a larg animal with a tail as long as their body.

Mountain lion

JUST THE FACTS!

Poisonous snakes? Nope, there are no poisonous snakes in Glacier National Park.

BIRDS: GLACIER'S FEATHERED FRIENDS

Chickadees, Nuthatches, and Brown Creepers: Traveling Companions

As you walk through fir and spruce forests, you frequently will hear the high-pitched, two-tone whistle of the chickadee calling its own name *(chickadee-dee-dee)*. Look in the direction from which the song comes and you will likely notice that the chickadee is not alone. It is traveling in a flock that might include other birds, such as nuthatches, brown creepers, juncos, and downy woodpeckers.

The reason the different species flock together is unclear, although there are a few theories. Perhaps it is for safety. When the members of one species become frightened, their actions alert the other birds of potential danger. Another explanation for the flocking behavior is that the diets of the birds are similar. Both nuthatches and brown creepers feed on the same food: insects concealed around the edges of tree bark. When you hear the characteristic chickadee's song, look for its traveling companions.

Brown creeper

Chickadee

Nuthatch

There are 294 species of birds in Montana, 260 of those are in Glacier.

Ruffed Grouse

You are walking through a forest that has dense undergrowth. Without warning, you hear a thunderous sound a few feet in front of you. Startled, you stop. Was that a bear?

No, you have just experienced a ruffed grouse beating its wings, trying to escape your presence. The grouse was aware you were coming. But the chicken-size bird is so "tame" that it did not get out of the way of potential danger until the last moment. As you watch what some people call a "fool-hen," you notice that it can't fly much better than a chicken. If it lands in a spruce tree, you will also notice it is not very good at standing in trees either!

Harlequin duck

THE LONG COMMUTE
The many colors and unusual patterns of its feathers identify this summer resident of the McDonald Creek Valley. The harlequin duck spends the winter on the coast diving for its food in the Pacific Ocean.

Ruffed grouse

Dippers

Look for bird droppings on the boulders in fast-moving creeks. These droppings tell you that dippers are living in the area. Listen for the *"zeet"* call. Dippers are gray, and about the size of a young robin with a short tail. They get their name from their bobbing behavior when standing on rocks. They build their nests out of mosses near fast-moving water, often behind waterfalls. Their strong yellow legs allow them to walk underwater in order to catch insects. Dippers are fun to watch as they walk into swiftly moving water and disappear. You can only guess where they will emerge.

Dipper   *Ptarmigan*

Ptarmigans

White as snow in winter but speckled brown in summer, the male ptarmigan (pronounced *TAR-mi-gan*) lives its life in the alpine regions of Glacier National Park. You may come across a ptarmigan on your hike to Hidden Lake Overlook. If you do, expect to be startled. They are so well camouflaged in the brush that they will flee danger only at the last moment, exploding into flight as they escape. The ptarmigan finds it easy to walk on soft fluffy snow because of the extra feathers on the tops and bottoms of its feet. These extra feathers make their feet into snowshoes. The scientific name for the ptarmigan means "hare-footed mountaineer."

Our National Symbol

Freedom, independence, and strength are represented in the American bald eagle. Glacier National Park is the home of many pairs of eagles during the summer. Bald eagles are mostly a fish-eating bird. Look for them along lakes and streams.

Bald eagle

Golden Eagles

Nowhere is this magnificent bird more majestic than when soaring over the eastern meadowlands, alpine tundra, and high peaks of the "Crown of the Continent," Glacier National Park. From these great heights, golden eagles hunt rabbits and large rodents, diving at blistering speed as they capture them in their talons.

Golde...

If you see an eagle perched you may be confused whether you are looking at an immature bald eagle or a golden eagle. Young bald eagles have not developed their characteristic white head. An immature bald eagle and a mature golden eagle may look alike. Instead, look at their legs! Golden eagles' legs are feathered down to the talons; bald eagles' legs are not.

Western meadowlark

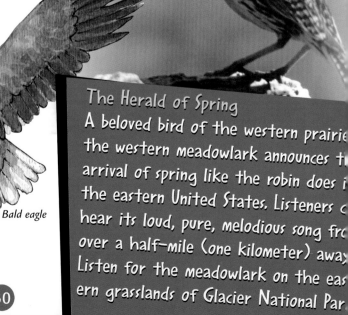

The Herald of Spring

A beloved bird of the western prairie the western meadowlark announces t... arrival of spring like the robin does i... the eastern United States. Listeners c... hear its loud, pure, melodious song fr... over a half-mile (one kilometer) away... Listen for the meadowlark on the eas... ern grasslands of Glacier National Par...

Raven   Pileated woodpecker   American kestrel

Brainy Bird

Ravens' intelligence is thought to be greater than that of dogs! Ravens can be confused with hawks as they glide gracefully high over the valleys of Glacier National Park. The large black birds can be identified when they are in flight by their wedge-shaped tail. They are predators and scavengers, willing to eat almost anything.

The Real Woody the Woodpecker

At 15 inches (38 centimeters), the pileated woodpecker is the largest woodpecker in North America. A year-round resident of Glacier National Park, it is located by listening for its slow drumming on trees and identified by the white patches on the undersides of its wings.

American Kestrel

The American kestrel is found in more places than any other bird that inhabits Glacier National Park. From Alaska to the tip of South America, this small falcon lives in open country, farmland, forest edges, and even cities. Sometimes called "sparrow hawks," they can be seen perched atop dead trees and posts in the meadows in the eastern part of Glacier. You might see one hovering overhead before it dives to capture small rodents or grasshoppers.

A CHECKLIST OF BIRDS:

- [ ] American kestrel
- [ ] bald eagle
- [ ] brown creeper
- [ ] chickadee
- [ ] dipper
- [ ] golden eagle
- [ ] harlequin duck
- [ ] nuthatch
- [ ] osprey
- [ ] pileated woodpecker
- [ ] ptarmigan
- [ ] raven
- [ ] ruffed grouse
- [ ] western meadowlark

What a Bully!

One of the most spectacular sights you will witness in Glacier National Park is an osprey carrying a fish from a lake back to its nest. Osprey are large predators, but strangely, the seemingly shy Canada goose will take over an osprey nest in the early spring. The goose will successfully fight to keep the osprey away while it uses the nest.

Osprey

SOMETHING'S FISHY IN GLACIER

Non-native fish that have been introduced to the waters of Glacier:

- rainbow trout
- brook trout
- kokanee salmon
- grayling
- Yellowstone cutthroat trout

Non-native fish destroy native fish populations by eating them, eating the native fishes' food, bringing diseases that the native fish can't fight, inter-breeding with native fish, or taking over a lake, river, or stream because they have no natural preda-tors in the new environment.

There are many kinds of fish in Glacier's waters, and they are either native (they exist in the park naturally) or non-native (they were brought to the park).

Until 1971, fish were raised in hatcheries outside the park and stocked—or placed—in many of the park's rivers and lakes. Many of these fish were non-native, and came from places like Yellowstone National Park, Minnesota, and even New York.

The practice of stocking fish has ended. Since 1971, Glacier National Park has worked to preserve the native fish populations and to keep non-native fish from invading the park. Some lakes and streams have original families of fish that go back 12,000 years! Since the last ice age! Some of the better-known species of fish native to these waterways are the westslope cutthroat trout, the mountain whitefish, and the bull trout.

Westslope cutthroat trout

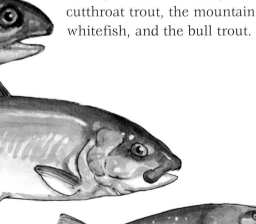

Mountain whitefish

Bull

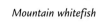

WHAT'S BUGGIN' YOU? GLACIER'S INSECTS

Although bears are large, powerful animals, among their favorite foods are two tiny insects: the army cutworm moth and the ladybug beetle.

Army Cutworm Moth

Army cutworm moths surface from the soil of the eastern Montana prairie in late June. Soon after, they fly to Glacier's rocky alpine meadows to escape the summer heat. At night, they feed on flowers; during the day they hide out under small rocks. Grizzly bears have learned that the moths are more nutritious than deer, and easier to catch. Lying on their bellies, and scooping with their paws, grizzly bears can eat as many as 40,000 moths per day. Look for overturned rocks and logs—a bear may have had a feast!

Army cutworm moth

Ladybug Beetle

Ladybug beetles fly from the prairies to the eastern and northern sides of the mountain peaks in September. Some rocks are covered so thickly with ladybugs that grizzly bears lick them up by the mouthful!

Most beetles eventually crawl under the rocks and go into hibernation until June. The deep snow on the mountains provides insulation against extreme cold. Prairie winters do not provide enough snow insulation for the ladybugs to survive the frigid temperatures. In June of the next year, the ladybugs return to the prairies.

Ladybug beetle

An Unwanted Souvenir

Mosquitoes abound in the Glacier National Park area during the warm months. You might find swarms of mosquitoes in the cool, damp areas as well as the warm, sunny hillsides.

What are they good for? Mosquitoes are important because they help pollinate plants.

Only female mosquitoes bite. They seek the protein in blood needed for their eggs to develop properly. Female mosquitoes are attracted to carbon dioxide. They can easily sense the gas you emit when you breathe.

If you plan to hike, you can protect yourself from mosquitoes by using insect repellents that contain citronella or 28-30 percent DEET, and by wearing protective clothing. Long sleeves, pants, and socks, as well as a bandanna tied around your neck that has been sprayed with repellent are most effective for keeping mosquitoes from biting. Even with all your precautions, if you do get a mosquito bite, just consider it a souvenir from Glacier National Park.

Mosquito

Mountain pine beetles

Beetles: Birds Love 'Em, Pine Trees Hate 'Em

The mountain pine beetle can be found throughout Glacier, especially in the low-lying areas where lodgepole pine trees grow. Pine beetles are slowly killing the trees by burrowing under the bark and eating their way around the tree.

Woodpeckers, on the other hand, find the beetles and their larvae nutritious, and they eat them in great numbers.

Infestations of mountain pine beetles have killed massive numbers of trees, leaving dead trees to dry out and become forest fire hazards. If you look closely in the North Fork area, you might see holes carved by woodpeckers searching for a meal of pine beetles.

UNINVITED PICNIC GUESTS!

Don't be surprised if your picnic is suddenly interrupted by a loud piercing screech resounding from a tree branch overhead. A deep-blue bird, with a black beak and a crest on its head, the Steller's jay has come to share lunch with you! The bird's repeated squawking will call even more jays to the party!

Or its cousin the gray jay, commonly known as a camp robber, may have an eye on your sandwich.

Another bird may boldly land close to your food. It is the size of the Steller's jay, without the crest, and is gray, white, and black. This is the Clark's nutcracker, and it also likes to join in on a meal.

The birds might distract you, but don't forget to watch your food! Small striped chipmunks and larger long-tailed squirrels have learned to quickly steal your food and scramble off into the bushes. Your relaxing picnic could easily become a competition!

Don't expect this to happen every time you stop to eat outside in Glacier, but it happens often. These animals are not tame, but they are accustomed to being around people. Birds and squirrels that live around picnic areas and campgrounds have learned that people leave bits and pieces of food behind. Because the animals are funny, cute, and entertaining, some people are willing to feed them.

Feeding wildlife leads to problems, though. The animals become dependent on handouts and see it as an easy source of food. The animals can then become a bother around picnic areas and campgrounds. Another problem is that animals carry diseases that can be contracted by humans. It is best not to get too close to some animals. Finally, when animals become dependent on handouts, they tend to ignore the food they get from the wild. Human food is meant for people only.

Golden-mantled ground squirrel

DO NOT FEED THE ANIMALS

Animals that rely on human food may become malnourished and unable to survive the winter. Keep your picnic area clean and remember, do not feed the animals!

Gray jay

IT'S OFFICIAL

The following are not allowed: feeding, touching, teasing, frightening, or intentionally disturbing of wildlife.

All the animals in Glacier National Park are wild. Wildlife can bite and they might carry diseases harmful to you. Feeding human food to animals denies them the nutrition they need to survive.

A WATER PARK!

Whether it is Lake McDonald—the largest body of water in Glacier National Park—or one of the smallest of the park's 561 streams, the park's waterways are teeming with life.

Glacier National Park has 653 lakes, covering 27,000 acres (10,935 hectares). The largest of these is Lake McDonald, at 10 miles long (16.1 kilometers) and 492 feet (150 meters) deep. The basin of Lake McDonald was carved by a huge glacier. Notice on the map that all the large lakes, such as Lake McDonald, Bowman, Kintla, Sherburne Lake, Two Medicine, and Saint Mary Lake, are long and narrow because they are in valleys cut by glaciers.

Kintla Lake
Bowman Lake
Quartz Lake
Lake Sherburne
Logging Lake
GOING-TO-THE-SUN ROAD
Lake McDonald
Saint Mary L:
Two Medicin
CONTINENTAL DIV

If you were to place all 561 of Glacier's rivers and streams end to end, they would stretch from Logan Pass to the Gulf of Mexico!

Tumbling Waters

It is impossible to count the number of waterfalls and cascades in Glacier National Park. Many of them are spectacular during spring thaw and active throughout the summer, but disappear as autumn nears. Most are fed by glaciers and melting snowfields. From almost anywhere you stand in Glacier National Park, you can see or hear water tumbling, as it slowly makes its way from the high mountains to an ocean.

Celebrated cascades along the Going-to-the-Sun Road are the Haystack and The Weeping Wall.

Notable waterfalls in Glacier are Running Eagle in the Two Medicine Valley, Bird Woman Falls, and Saint Mary Falls and Virginia Falls along the Going-to-the-Sun Road.

The Weeping Wall

Running Eagle Falls

Hidden Lake Overlook

WHAT'S THE DIFFEREN

Waterfall or casca
A cascade is water
that flows downhi
and is always in
contact with a
surface of rocks.
A waterfall is wate
that falls freely
from a rock surface

FABULOUS FIELDS OF FLOWERS

Glacier National Park is famous for its wildflowers that bloom throughout the summer and into autumn. The reason is that Glacier is a "vertical park," a park with many elevations.

Generally, for every 100 feet (30 meters) in elevation gain, the plants are delayed in blooming by about one day. Glacier lilies that bloom on the McDonald Valley floor in May will not bloom at Logan Pass until July. Because of this, plants seem to be in bloom in the park thoughout the summer and into autumn.

Perennial or Annual?

Most of the flowering plants in Glacier are perennials. Perennials are plants that stay alive over the winter and bloom year after year, as opposed to annuals, which are plants that die each winter. Perennials do not go through their life cycle in one growing season. They do not have to germinate from seed, grow roots, and grow leaves, like annuals have to do each spring. When spring arrives, perennials already have roots, stems, and leaves. The plant is ready to flower and to produce seeds.

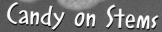
Huckleberries

Candy on Stems

Huckleberries are an important food for black bears and grizzly bears. The fruit ripens from August to mid-September. The bears depend on the high sugar content in the berries to help them put on fat for winter hibernation. If pregnant bears do not get enough sugar from the huckleberries, they will give birth to fewer cubs. If you see bears foraging in the avalanche chutes in the Many Glacier Valley, they are likely gorging themselves on huckleberries.

A Feast of Glacier Lilies

Also known as snow lilies, the glacier lilies recede up the valleys as the snow melts. You will see them blooming next to patches of snow. Look for large fields of glacier lilies at Logan Pass. The underground bulbs are eaten by rodents, black bears, and grizzly bears. The above-ground seedpods are eaten by deer, elk, bighorn sheep, and mountain goats.

Glacier lilies

WANTED: DEAD, NOT ALIVE

Spotted knapweed

Early settlers deliberately brought some plants to Glacier National Park, and other plants began growing in Glacier because their seeds were attached to automobiles or in hay used to feed horses. These non-native flowering plants, such as spotted knapweed, are invasive, taking over meadows and hillsides, and using water needed by the native plants. They crowd out the native plants that animals need for their survival. The National Park Service is attempting to remove some of the most dangerous invasive plant species from the park, but you will still see some non-native flowering plants along the roadways and trails.

Blazing Fireweed

Fireweed is a perennial that will turn a blackened landscape into a sea of color during the first summer after a fire. The plants spread rapidly, placing nutrients in the fire-affected ground. You will also see fireweed along the roads and trails in Glacier National Park, where other plants will not grow.

Fire...

Nature's Paintbrush

The paintbrush plant is named for its colorful ragged flower. You will find this showy perennial along the Going-to-the-Sun Road, Two Medicine Road, and Many Glacier Road. Hummingbirds love paintbrush nectar.

Paintb...

Bunches of Bear Grass

You will find hillsides completely covered in bear grass blooms during some summer seasons. Individual plants do not bloom every year but instead on a 3- to 10-year cycle. If you are fortunate, you will see a whole population of bear grass blooming at the same time. Bears sometimes snack on the leaves in the springtime; rodents, elk, and bighorn sheep eat the flowers and seedpods.

Bear...

THE TREES OF GLACIER'S FORESTS

Glacier National Park is home to many kinds of tress. They can be found in many areas, including:

- **the eastern parklands**
- **the North Fork Valley bottom**
- **the subalpine zone**
- **the McDonald Creek Valley**

Each is identifiable by the trees that dominate that zone.

The Eastern Parklands

The open spaces and prairies on the eastern side of Glacier National Park are called parklands.

Earthquake?

The dominant tree in the parklands is the quaking aspen. You will find large groves of aspens in the Saint Mary, Many Glacier, Belly River, and Two Medicine areas. Visit Saint Mary campground and stand within the aspen grove. The slightest breeze shows why the trees are called quaking aspens, as their leaves quiver and shake.

Quaking aspens are deciduous trees, which means they lose their leaves each year. Just before they fall off, the leaves turn a brilliant yellow.

The North Fork Valley Bottom

This zone is a broad flood plain of the North Fork of the Flathead River. It includes the river bottom and the shoulder of the Livingston Range of mountains. It has a wide variety of tree species; three dominant ones include the ponderosa pine, lodgepole pine, and the western larch.

Butterscotch Trees

The ponderosa pine is the state tree of Montana. Older ponderosas are sometimes called yellowbellies because of the color of their trunks. Approach a ponderosa pine tree on a warm, windless day and smell the trunk. What does the fragrance remind you of? Some people can smell vanilla; others say they smell butterscotch. Ponderosa pine trees can survive many fires throughout their long lives. Fire benefits ponderosa pine communities by removing plants and trees that compete for water and nutrients in the soil.

Tepee Trees

Lodgepole pines are fast-growing, slender trees that are used as poles for tepees (sometimes called lodges). They could be called tepee trees! The trees are easily killed by fire, but they need forest fires in order to reproduce. Their cones remain closed on the trees for many years. Forest fires open the pine cones and allow the seeds to fall to the freshly burned forest floor. Lodgepole pines are one of the first trees to start a new forest after a fire.

Lodgepole pines

Western larch

Western Larch

The western larch is one of only three cone-bearing tree species that lose their needles each autumn. The needles turn bright yellow, then golden in October. By December, all of the needles have fallen. It is a spectacular sight to see the golden larch trees mixed in with evergreens like ponderosa pines and lodgepole pines. The other two pine trees that lose their needles each year are the bald cypress of the southeastern United States and the dawn redwood of northern China.

Subalpine Zone— The High Country

Trees of the subalpine forests characterize the upper reaches of Glacier National Park: subalpine firs, Engelmann's spruce, and whitebark pine. A walk around the visitor center at Logan Pass will introduce you to these three trees, which appear miniature because of the constant wind and winter ice. Shrubby forms of Engelmann's spruce and subalpine firs bunched together are known as krummholz. You can "feel" Glacier's extreme weather by just looking at an island of these stunted trees.

Whiteba

The McDonald Creek Valley

The mountains that divide Glacier National Park from north to south capture rainfall on the western slopes. McDonald Creek Valley is characterized by groves of western red cedar and western hemlock. The Trail of the Cedars near Avalanche Campground is an excellent place to see the red cedars and hemlock trees that make up this wet forest environment. Cedar and hemlock forests have little direct sunlight reaching the ground and are cool, with thick undergrowth. Some of the trees along the trail are more than 500 years old!

Trail of the C

GLACIER ON FIRE!

For most of the history of Glacier National Park, park managers and scientists viewed fire as a bad event. Recently, they have looked upon the role of fire in forests and grasslands through different eyes.

Why Some Fires Aren't Put Out

Fires are a natural part of the environment, just as natural as rain and snow.

Restraining natural fires can be bad for the environment. Stopping some fires means that the materials that should burn do not. These burnable materials build up in the forest and grasslands until they become dangerous. When a fire starts, it will burn at too hot a temperature and can occur in areas with young plants—areas not yet ready to burn.

The forest and grassland panorama you now see in Glacier was shaped by fire. Every part of Glacier has burned at some time.

American Indians regularly burned the grasslands of Glacier in order to improve animal habitat and keep trees from growing.

Lightning-caused fires burn every year in the park. Since 1988, Glacier has averaged 14 fires each summer, affecting about 5,000 acres (2,024 hectares) per year.

There probably will be a couple of fires burning in the park during your visit, but you may be unaware of it. Because the small fires are in remote areas, you may not see flames or smoke. These are watched by park service fire specialists to make sure they do not become a threat to buildings or people.

Moose walking on a fire line

What Happens to the Animals?

The vision that cartoons portray of animals panicking before a forest fire is not supported by firefighter observations.

Many firefighters tell stories about seeing deer, elk, and moose foraging within a few feet of a ground fire. Large animals simply move away to escape the flames. Firefighters rarely report finding dead deer, elk, moose, bighorn sheep, mountain goats, or bears. Smaller animals go underground or are killed. Birds fly or walk away from the flames.

What Happens to the Plants?

Lightning-caused fires are a natural event that many plant and animal populations need in order to be healthy. Fires reduce grasses, trees, and shrubs to ash, releasing nutrients into the soil.

Lodgepole pine trees, huckleberries, and fireweed need fire in order to reproduce. The heat of the fire causes huckleberry and fireweed seeds to start to grow. It also causes lodgepole pine cones to pop open, releasing seeds.

Some forests burn every 50 to 80 years; some grasslands should burn every autumn in order to remain healthy.

GLACIER ON ICE!

You may ask: Do people come here in the winter? How do the flowers survive? What happens to the animals?

Snowfall

Glacier National Park is a large park with a landscape that varies from high rocky alpine mountaintops to low-lying meadows. More snow tends to fall in the high elevations. Half of the park is west of the Continental Divide and receives a lot of snow, while the half east of the Divide receives less snow. Some areas of the park will receive as little as a few inches of snow over the winter, while others will receive many feet of snow. Averaging all the areas out, the amount of snow that falls in Glacier during the winter months is 11 feet (3.3 meters), with most of the snow falling in December and January.

> In Glacier National Park, it can snow in every month of the year.

Glacier National Park, looking south toward Great Bear Wilderness

JUST THE FACTS!

Brrr!
The maximum low temperature in the park is −36 degrees Fahrenheit (−38 degrees Celsius)!

Ranger and kids watching wildlife in winter

Plants and Animals in Winter

We think of lots of snow and very cold temperatures as describing a severe winter. Glacier's plants and animals are adapted to winter conditions that some people think are unbearable. Plants and animals, such as the rock rabbit, ptarmigan, and gray wolf, are adapted to living during Glacier's winter weather.

Long-lived perennial plants have stored enough nourishment in their roots and stems to allow them to start growing when the winter is over.

Many animals rest through the cold season in hibernation underneath the snow. Other animals stay active during the winter months looking for food and seeking shelter from storms when necessary.

Pikas

Pikas, also known as rock rabbits, need the cool air of the alpine region. Pikas thrive in temperatures that we call frigid, but they live only a few hours in temperatures we think of as comfortable (77 degrees Fahrenheit, 25 degrees Celsius). The rock jumbles that they call home provide protection from what we would think of as a mild temperature.

Ptarmigans

Deep snow may be a problem for us, but not for the feathered ptarmigans. They burrow into the snow to stay warm. Snow has an insulating effect. The ptarmigan fluffs its feathers to make a little cavern in the snow. Its body heat keeps the air warm within the cavern, while the temperature of the air just a few inches above may be several degrees colder.

Gray Wolves

Gray wolves don't mind the snow and cold weather. They have an easier time catching prey like the white-tailed deer when the snow is deep enough to slow the deer's escape.

White ptarmigan in snow

COOL HIKES FOR KIDS

Glacier is an excellent park for hiking. From the trail, you can experience the beauty of the birds and mammals, enjoy the sounds of running water, feel the wind on your face, and smell the wildflowers and the forests. There are several short hikes in the park that will make your stay more fun.

Are we there yet?

Swiftcurrent Lake Trail

Many Glacier Area

Roundtrip distance: 2.6 miles, 4.2 kilometers.

Time: 2 hours.

Best time of the year: June–October.

Trailhead: You can begin this trail at the south end of the Many Glacier Hotel or at the Many Glacier Picnic Area.

Hike halfway around Swiftcurrent Lake to the paved trail to Lake Josephine. It is an extra 0.2-mile walk to the beautiful high mountain lake. The hike around Swiftcurrent Lake to Lake Josephine is through moose and bear country. Make noise so they can hear you on the trail!

Trail of the Cedars

Along the Going-to-the-Sun Road

Roundtrip distance: 0.7 miles, 1.1 kilometers.

Time: 1 hour.

Best time of the year: June–September.

Trailhead: The trailhead is immediately east of Avalanche Creek Campground along the Going-to-the-Sun Road.

Trail of the Cedars is the most popular loop trail in Glacier National Park. The hike leads you along Avalanche Creek, through an old forest of huge western red cedar and hemlock trees. Some of the cedar trees were more than 100 years old by the time our nation was founded in 1776. The smaller trees with drooping tops are mountain hemlocks.

The first half of the trail is on a boardwalk; it then turns into a footpath after crossing the footbridge over Avalanche Creek. Look for dippers along the creek. The bobbing of these birds in the water is very entertaining!

BE CAREFUL!

Rocks and streambanks can be unstable, so please use care along streams and lakes and near waterfalls.

Swiftcurrent Lake Trail

Forests and Fire Nature Trail

North Fork Road

Roundtrip distance:
0.9 miles, 1.4 kilometers.

Time: 1 hour.

Best time of the year:
June–October.

Trailhead: Between the Camas Creek entrance station and the Glacier National Park entrance sign.

This trail is often called the Huckleberry Mountain Nature Trail. Forest fires have burned this area in the 1960s and again in 2001. Can you still smell the burned forest? It is a wonderful trail that shows the importance of fire to the plants and animals of Glacier.

Running Eagle Falls

Along the Two Medicine Road

Roundtrip distance:
0.6 miles, 1 kilometer.

Time: 1 hour.

Best time of the year: July–September.

Trailhead: The trailhead is one mile (1.6 kilometers) west of the Two Medicine entrance station.

Running Eagle Falls used to be called Trick Falls. It got the name Trick Falls because the water falls both over the top of a cliff and out of a cave. Before the middle of July, there may be enough water falling from the cliff to cover up the water coming out of the cave. By late September you may see water only coming out of the cave.

Where is everyone?

Baring Falls Trail

Baring Falls

Saint Mary Lake

Roundtrip distance: 1.4 miles, 2.2 kilometers.

Time: 1 hour.

Best time of the year: June–October.

Trailhead: The trailhead is at the southeast corner of the large Sun Point parking lot off Going-to-the-Sun Road. The trail follows the Sun Point Nature Trail.

This is a beautiful and historical area. Follow the trail as it goes to Saint Mary Lake and along the lakeshore to Baring Falls. Along the way you will pass the place where the Great Northern Railway built the Going-to-the-Sun Chalets in 1913. The area had nine buildings, including a main lodge, an employee living space, and guest sleeping quarters. The chalet was removed in 1949.

You will arrive at Baring Falls after about 30 minutes of hiking. Baring Falls was once called Water Ouzel Falls because of the water ouzels or dippers living there. Look for dippers flying, wading, and bobbing near the waterfall.

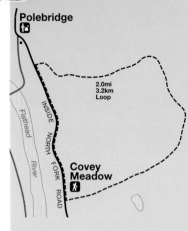

Covey Meadow Loop

Polebridge Area
Roundtrip distance:
2.0 miles, 3.2 kilometers.
Time: 1 hour.
Best time of the year:
July–October.
Trailhead: The trailhead is 0.5 miles, 0.9 kilometers, south of the Polebridge entrance station on the Inside North Fork Road.

The trail goes through a forest affected by the Red Bench Fire of September 1988. Notice the uniform height of the lodgepole pines that have grown since the fire. A group of trees growing this closely together is called "dog-hair." The trail goes through part of Covey Meadow, which is part of an old creek bed. From the meadow, you will see the Livingston Range, and you might also see elk, deer, bears, foxes, coyotes, squirrels, and many kinds of birds.

Hidden Lake Overlook

Logan Pass
Roundtrip distance:
4.0 miles, 6.4 kilometers.
Time: 2 hours.
Best time of the year: July–October.
Trailhead: The trailhead is directly behind the Logan Pass Visitor Center.

Don't miss this hike! This trail to the Hidden Lake overlook gives you one of the most spectacular scenic views in the park. The trail is partly boardwalk, partly paved, and in some places, unpaved gravel. The trail goes through high alpine fields of flowers and over ice-cold streamlets. Along the way, you may encounter mountain goats, bighorn sheep, chipmunks, and Columbian ground squirrels. Be sure to take a jacket. It can be very cold and windy at the overlook.

Rainbow Falls

Goat Haunt Area
Roundtrip distance:
2.0 miles, 3.2 kilometers.
Time: 2 hours.
Best time of the year:
June–September.
Trailhead: You will need to take the excursion boat from Waterton Township to the end of Waterton Lake. The trailhead is next to the ranger station.

This is an easy, short, and pleasant hike though a lodgepole pine forest. The trail ends at the top of the waterfall. Rainbow Falls is more like a long cascade with several beautiful blue pools. Ask your parents to check at the ranger station to see what identification is required to cross the U.S./Canada border.

Horseback riding is a grea[t]
to see Glacier National P[ark]

BE A JUNIOR RANGER!

If you are between the ages of 6 and 12, you can become a Junior Ranger by completing the family activities found in the Junior Ranger Newspaper. This newspaper is available at all of the Glacier National Park visitor centers.

There is also an education cabin located near the Apgar Visitor Center. The center is designed to allow you and your family to explore educational and fun activities. Look for the park newspaper section "Glacier Explorer" for current programs and schedules. Be sure to check this out early during your visit—preferably the first day—so you can earn a Junior Ranger Badge!

You will need to complete several requirements during your vacation. These may include:

- Complete at least five of the seven activities in the Junior Ranger activity book.
- Attend a ranger-led program.
- Hike one of the park's trails.
- Review the park's rules about staying away from wild animals, not feeding them, not picking wildflowers, staying on boardwalks and trails, and so on—rules anyone visiting Glacier should learn.
- Explain in a short sentence or two why you want to be a Junior Ranger.
- Read and understand the Junior Ranger Pledge.
- Show on a map the places in Glacier you visit.

All of the activities present different challenges. Some must be accomplished outdoors. Other activities can be done even while waiting for a restaurant meal, riding in the car, or during the evenings in a lodge or at your campsite.

When you become 18, you can join the Student Conservation Association (SCA). The SCA is the nation's leading provider of conservation service opportunities, outdoor skills, and leadership training for youth. Every year, high school and college students work on projects in Glacier National Park that might include visitor services, such as interpreting the park's natural and cultural history through talks and guided hikes, working at an information desk, or assisting with resource management programs. Contact SCA at www.thesca.org.

Some day you may want to embark on a career as a National Park Service Ranger. There are many different ways to prepare for a job as a ranger. Earning your Junior Ranger Badge is a good beginning. The Association of National Park Rangers also publishes a guide called "Live the Adventure: Join the National Park Service." The guide costs $5 and will give you good information on how to become a ranger. Order the guide by visiting www.anpr.org/park-ranger.htm.

ABOUT THE AUTHOR

Alan Leftridge has been a seasonal ranger/naturalist in Yellowstone National Park and a wilderness ranger in the Mission Mountains Wilderness Area of Montana. He earned a bachelor's degree in biology at Central Missouri State University, a doctorate in science education at Kansas State University, and a teaching credential from the University of Montana. Since 1973, he taught high school science in West Yellowstone, science courses at Miami University in Ohio, and environmental studies classes at Humboldt State University in California. He is currently the executive editor of *The Interpreter* magazine of the National Association for Interpretation, has authored *Glacier Day Hikes*, published in 2003 by Farcountry Press in Helena, Montana, and self published *Seeley-Swan Day Hikes*, in 2005. Alan lives south of Glacier National Park in the Swan Valley and conducts interpretive writing workshops and Certified Interpretive Guide training around the country. www.leftridge.com

Visitors on boardwalk

Special Thanks to Judy Stewart's fourth-grade class at Ruder Elementary School in Columbia Falls, Montana, for their suggestions for this book!